VickiB .

D1474552

RECENT BOOKS IN THE MERCIFULLY BRIEF, REAL WORLD SERIES

Raising More Money With Newsletters
Than You Ever Thought Possible
by Tom Ahern • Emerson & Church, Publishers • $24.95

Today, countless organizations are raising more money with their newsletter than with traditional mail appeals. In *Raising More Money With Newsletters Than You Ever Thought Possible*, Tom Ahern shows why.

"Almost every donor newsletter I see suffers from at least one of seven fatal flaws," he says early in the book. Eliminate these flaws and your returns will soar.

Raising $1,000 Gifts by Mail
by Mal Warwick • Emerson & Church, Publishers • $24.95

Whoever heard of raising $1,000 gifts (not to mention $3,000, $4,000, and $5,000 gifts) by mail? That's the realm of personal solicitation, right? Not exclusively says Mal Warwick in his book, *Raising $1,000 Gifts by Mail*.

With carefully selected examples and illustrations, Warwick shows you how to succeed with high dollar mail, walking you step by step through the process of identifying your prospects, crafting the right letter, the right brochure, the right response device, and the right envelope.

The Mercifully Brief, Real World Guide to ...

Attracting the Attention Your Cause Deserves

Emerson & Church
Real World Guides

Copyright 2005, by Joseph Barbato

All right reserved.

No portion of this book may be reproduced or used in any form, or by any means, without prior written permission from the publisher. Exceptions are made for brief excerpts used in published reviews.

First printed September 2005

10 9 8 7 6 5 4 3 2 1

Printed in the United States of America

This text is printed on acid-free paper.

Emerson & Church, Publishers
P.O. Box 338, Medfield, MA 02052
Tel. 508-359-0019
Fax 508-359-2703
www.emersonandchurch.com

Copies of this book are available from the publisher at discount when purchased in quantity for boards of directors or staff.

Library of Congress Cataloging-in-Publication Data

Barbato, Joseph, 1944-
  The mercifully brief, real world guide to -- attracting the attention your cause deserves / Joseph Barbato.
     p. cm.
   ISBN 1-889102-06-7 (pbk. : alk. paper)
  1. Publicity. 2. Nonprofit organizations--Management. I. Title.
   HM1226.B37 2005
   659.2'88--dc22
                              2005022343

The Mercifully Brief,
Real World Guide to ...

Attracting the Attention Your Cause Deserves

JOSEPH BARBATO

Emerson
& Church
PUBLISHERS

ALSO BY JOSEPH BARBATO

HOW TO WRITE KNOCKOUT PROPOSALS
What You Must Know (And Say)
To Win Funding Every Time

WRITING FOR A GOOD CAUSE
The Complete Guide to Crafting Proposals
and Other Persuasive Pieces for Nonprofits
(with Danielle S. Furlich)

OFF THE BEATEN PATH
Stories of Place
(with Lisa Weinerman Horak)

PATCHWORK OF DREAMS
Voices from the Heart of the New America
(with Morty Sklar)

HEART OF THE LAND
Essays on Last Great Places
(with Lisa Weinerman)

YOU ARE WHAT YOU DRINK
The Authoritative Report on What Alcohol
Does to Your Body, Mind, and Longevity
(with Allan Luks)

For Dusty

Without publicity, a terrible thing happens: Nothing.

– P.T. Barnum

CONTENTS

PREFACE

Years ago I directed publicity for a small New York City college. The college had opened only a few years before, and I was the first person to give focused thought to publicizing its programs.

It was a community college for working class students, most of them recent immigrants who worked in offices and factories in Manhattan, lived in the densely populated neighborhoods of western Queens, and were trying to improve themselves by taking evening classes.

As La Guardia Community College's first public information director, I could have begun issuing press releases about unusual courses and faculty. Instead, I did something far more prosaic. I arranged to have signs with the college's name installed on the platforms of the nearby subway station.

It was a start.

The college was hidden away in a Long Island City, Queens, industrial district. Most New Yorkers had never heard of it. Few passengers on the Flushing IRT subway line realized that a school meeting their needs was conveniently located in a converted factory building just a short walk from the Rawson Street subway station. And yet this was New York City, where many residents base their mental picture of the urban landscape on signage at subway stops – "81st Street – Museum of Natural History," "8th Street – New York University," "Brooklyn Bridge – City Hall," "161st Street – Yankee Stadium," and so on.

The people taking the Flushing IRT train were our prospective students. As a native New Yorker, I knew it was essential they see the words "Rawson Street-LaGuardia Community College" when they pulled into "our" station. The signs went up. They remain there to this day.

In this book I'll tell you how to get the word out – and the signs up – about your organization. I assume you're a busy executive who wants to heighten the visibility of a nonprofit. Unlike the president of Harvard University, you can't pick up your phone and talk to a vice president for external relations who can ask a director of public relations to have the manager of media relations get an announcement out. You have little or no staff. You have all you can do to keep programs going and make your operating budget. Publicity is not a priority.

And yet.

You know you could be taking action to boost your numbers, attract donors, win friends in the community, and pave the way for your future plans. And the action involves *getting publicity*. Or, to be more precise, getting publicity *now*.

Although you may lack public relations experience, you would like to know what you can do – with little time or budget – to publicize your cause. You want to take *action*, not engage in *activities*. You want to learn effective ways to maximize your group's potential for winning increased visibility. And you want to have this summarized in an economical book.

I've written *Attracting the Attention Your Cause Deserves* for you. This guide distills the essence of my experience working for nonprofit groups, both large and small, in efforts that garnered publicity in media from local newspapers to *The Wall Street Journal* and *The New York Times*, and in many magazines, newsletters, and broadcast outlets. It won't give you the addresses of magazine writers or Internet bloggers you may want to reach – those are readily available elsewhere. Here you'll find the vital steps you must take to make sure you have something to say when you finally have a reporter on the phone line.

What is your organization's niche? What makes it special? What are its strengths and main programs? How do you talk about yourself? What is your story? What is exciting, different, colorful, news worthy about you? Who do you want to reach with your message? What is the best way to do that?

This book covers these essentials and more. I've personally used the action steps described here to successfully publicize the work of many nonprofit groups – from a major research university to a local alcohol and drug prevention agency to a national literary organization. No matter what your cause, you can use the same clear-cut, practical, realistic approaches to win new visibility among audiences that matter to you.

Let's get started.

Alexandria, Virginia   Joseph Barbato

1

Sharpen Your Niche

Your phone rings, and the caller says he's with the American Red Cross. He's a stranger, but you know something about him already. He's with a credible and praiseworthy organization that's done good work helping victims of disasters from hurricanes to the terror attacks of 9/11.

If your caller was from the New York Public Library or the Mayo Clinic, you'd know a bit about him too. You'd feel comfortable taking the call. These are institutions that have won public recognition and trust.

What do people think when *you* call? Do you have to explain what your organization does? Must you do so at length? Does that trouble you? It should.

Not every nonprofit can be world renowned. Few are. But when you reach out to talk to the movers and shakers who matter to you, you don't want them to say, *Huh?* If they do, you have a problem. You need a higher public profile. And getting that profile is hard unless you have a specific niche.

Your niche is that highly focused corner of society where you do your thing. The Red Cross saves lives. Amnesty International safeguards human rights. The Getty Museum showcases great art. Well-known organizations generally do one thing very well. That one thing may have many components. But it forms a secure and overarching niche.

If your organization's work has a scattershot quality – if it does a little of this, some of that, and a few things in particular – that's not surprising.

Organizations evolve and add new programs over time. Often their growth is opportunistic – not strategic. They may drift from their missions, wander down tangential lanes, and find themselves engaged in activities that, well, don't really fit their main purpose.

I'm reminded of a client that served the health information needs of Latinos across the country. That was a pretty tight niche in itself. But as time passed the group expanded its programs in response to new opportunities. They began offering classes on employment, housing, legal, and other issues of concern to their audience.

All organizations do it. But each new initiative took the health group further and further away from its central purpose. Now, they have to *explain* why they do certain things.

If your organization is at such a point, it may be time to refocus your niche. That process lies outside the scope of this book and requires the help of experienced marketing consultants. Sometimes it entails changing your name – a major step. Or maybe you have to look at your programs and determine which really matter – which ones are making a significant contribution. Maybe some should be folded into others.

Fortunately, most organizations don't need a complete overhaul to sharpen their niche. They just have to trim a few loose ends to get sleek and simple – and memorable.

When you have a well-defined niche, good things happen. The next editor you call will already know exactly what you do. His only question will be what great story you're bringing him about *that*.

Hone your niche. It will grease the skid for your publicity successes.

2

Take Inventory

What does your organization do? I mean really *do*? Chances are, you think you know, but don't.

Sure, your membership brochure outlines some key program areas. But your website and annual reports talk about new directions. And your newsletter keeps reporting on events that depart from your traditional offerings of just a few years ago.

In today's society, change occurs at the speed of an instant message. Quite possibly, so much has changed about your organization – as you try to accommodate the evolving needs of the people you serve – that you're not really talking to the media about who you now are.

Given a big budget, you could do an entire branding exercise, including focus groups and in-depth research to identify your particular hook. Without doubt, that sort of expensive undertaking can help. But you can hone in on your group's identity just as easily by taking a few simple steps.

A relatively simple one is to engage a small group of trusted board and staff members in the process of taking inventory (if you can recruit a public relations expert, pro bono, all the better).

This group of a half dozen or so people serves as an investigative team. Their aim is to examine all aspects of your organization's activities and pinpoint the outstanding services that define its main role and contribution to the field.

Their tasks include:

• Reading key printed materials of the past few years. What is the organization saying about itself in its annual report, newsletters, and press releases? What would an outside person think are its main strengths?

• Visiting a range of the organization's programs and talking with participants. What's special about the programs? How do participants benefit? How do the programs touch their lives?

• Interviewing key staff and board members as well as outsiders, including foundation heads and corporate donors, who know the organization well - asking each to describe what comes to mind when thinking about the organization. What do they admire about it? Why?

I've engaged in this process with many clients, and the results are often surprising. Some discover that their current printed materials describe one conception of their organization – the idealized (and near-obsolete) one of yore. Further, on-site program visits reveal new directions that have changed the group's identity considerably. And interviews with key figures sometimes show that the organization isn't touting its real strengths.

I remember listening to the divergent takes on the work of a Washington, D.C. think tank from two of its board members. One thought the group's policy papers were having a significant impact in shaping the nation's energy policies. The other lamented the think tank's inconsequential efforts to shape policy, but was excited about its role as a catalyst for the broad energy community. As it happens, serving as a catalyst for others through seminars and conferences had in fact surpassed the group's direct contribution to policy making.

Failure to recognize what your organization does best can limit your ability to tell your story. If *you* lack a clear understanding of what matters, what is a journalist to think when you come calling?

3

Who Benefits?

You probably think you know who benefits from your organization's work. After all, if you provide training, your students benefit. If you care for the sick, your patients benefit. That's simple enough.

Perhaps too simple.

One afternoon I led board members of a regional theater in a discussion of the "values" offered by their program. We quickly decided that staging performances was one chief value. Clearly, audiences benefited. But then we discovered we offered value to people in other ways.

Someone noted that the theater encouraged new playwrights and trained young people in stagecraft. At a time when serious theater was losing ground to other forms of entertainment, wasn't this a service to the larger theatrical community? Indeed it was.

Then we thought about all the men and women who traveled from throughout the region to attend our plays and musical performances. The regional theater was a destination for many people – and brought money into the state's economy. That meant the entire state benefited.

Most organizations meet the needs of several constituencies. Knowing who benefits is key to understanding your group and its contributions to the community. Moreover, these constituencies are made up of the very people you want to reach through your publicity efforts.

A local hospital certainly delivers benefits to sick people and their families. But if it's one of the largest employers in town – as many hospitals are – it's also crucial to the local economy.

The same hospital benefits local employers: it helps keep employees healthy and on the job. It may also do outreach work in diabetes prevention (which keeps people out of sickbeds), in drug education (which keeps youths off drugs and in school), and so on.

Education programs don't simply impart information for the personal benefit of students. They empower people to become productive citizens in their communities. They provide skilled workers for business and industry. They too can be major employers. The University of Virginia, for example, is the largest provider of jobs in Charlottesville, VA. That's true of large nonprofits in many towns.

Your organization may offer value to a half dozen constituencies, both small and large. They are your market. If they are to act on your behalf, you must keep them in the publicity loop.

4

Make a Plan

Even if you haven't been through a branding exercise, or developed a strategic plan, you'll still want to devise some sort of plan for your publicity efforts based on your mission and what you've learned in researching the strengths of your organization.

What strategies will you use to reach key audiences? What goals will you set for yourself? "More press coverage" is too vague. A specific and measurable goal would be making two major placements in the next four months in media targeted at a key audience.

Your plan should take into account all communications efforts – not only media relations but also your website, print publications, and any other informational efforts aimed at key audiences. As much as possible, integrate all of these so that audiences receive your major stories in various media at about the same time.

In a small way, you'll be doing the same thing Hollywood producers do when they promote a new blockbuster movie. They make sure we see previews in TV advertisements, hear actors promoting the film on talk shows, read behind-the-scenes features in the newsweeklies, and find action figures based on the movie characters on sale at fast food restaurants.

On a far smaller scale, with your own audiences, you can make sure all your coverage occurs in the same timeframe – from appearances on local TV to website and newsletter stories to newspaper coverage and editorials.

As a rule of thumb, your communications plan might include:

- Overview – why publicity is needed and how it will support the mission of your organization

- Goals – what should publicity help accomplish: increased attendance or enrollment, greater awareness among prospective donors, impact on policy-making?

- Key messages – the main points you want to make

- Strategies and tactics – the reasoning behind your overall approach and the best vehicles for your messages

- Budget – how much money do you need and where will it come from?

- Timetable – dates by which specific actions will take place

- Evaluation – a method for determining what difference the publicity made

Needless to say, you'll want to revisit your communications plan regularly, if only because the media landscape is always changing. Before you know it, the new web log or business magazine launched six months ago can become a key place for reaching prospective supporters.

5

Staying on Message

In an ideal world, a reporter with a question could call six different offices within your organization and get the same answer. All of your staff would be "on message." Each person would have the same view and the same understanding of what matters, including the informed answer to the reporter's question.

Are you smiling? You should be. In the typical nonprofit, a reporter would probably get a mix of answers to any one question. But it doesn't have to be that way.

At some organizations, all staff members are expected to be fundraisers. That is, they're supposed to be well-informed advocates for the organization. They know the group's mission, its major programs, its positions on key issues. They're encouraged to share their passion for the cause with friends and neighbors, in talks at community gatherings, and in other ways.

That may be more than you can expect from your staff, but to the extent you can emulate this approach it makes for a powerful marketing machine. Each employee becomes an extension of the organization's advancement efforts.

That kind of magic can occur when an organization takes pains to know itself, and then conveys that knowledge to its staff and board. Once *you* understand your strengths, you can help keep everyone in house on message

By making effective use of in-house communications, you can give priority programs the same major exposure *inside* your organization that you want to obtain for them in outside media. Newsletters, e-mail updates, bulletin boards, staff meetings, and organizational retreats are useful vehicles for keeping everybody informed about achievements that exemplify the high quality work you do in your niche.

In some enterprises, the process of keeping everyone on message is much more deliberate. When controversies arise, recent Presidential administrations have made it a practice to issue "talking points" to all cabinet members to ensure "message discipline." That way, when a reporter calls around asking for comments on an issue, he hears a chorus of voices singing off the same page of a hymnal.

Senior executives at Wal-Mart, the country's largest corporation, appear in video broadcasts to the stores each week. They discuss everything from what merchandise to highlight to messages relating to the Wal-Mart reputation. Why? To keep employees knowledgeable and feeling positive about the company, and to empower them to deliver Wal-Mart's messages to friends, neighbors, and others.

You are the best judge of what will work at your organization. Somewhere along the continuum from sharing information to issuing suggested talking points, there lies a way to help key staff members understand the things that matter.

6

Be Clear. Be Concise. Be Gone.

What is the "nut" of your story? The classic 5 W's – who, what, where, when and why – are still what matters. Why then do so many organizations shovel gobs of useless information at reporters?

The impulse seems to be universal. Many nonprofits will mail reporters lengthy pitch letters with elaborate press kits filled with background sheets, suggested interview questions, headshots, clips, and other materials.

Press kits have their place. But they aren't meant to be crammed with detritus and used to whack journalists over the head. There are just so many 20-minute videos you can expect a reporter to watch in the newsroom.

Like you, most reporters are busy, multi-tasking people. Many are overworked and underpaid. Editors are after them to turn stories in.

As a result, you want to make a newsperson's work *easier* – not harder. A succinct powerful paragraph or two will get your story idea far more focused attention than a pile of paper.

If you're sending a press release, be certain your writing is as clear and concise as possible. Turgid sentences in thick paragraphs filled with complex concepts aren't going to grab a reporter who has to riffle through a stack of mail before jumping in his car to cover a fire.

If you're going to be writing releases and other material for the media, read Strunk and White's *The Elements of Style*, a small classic covering the most common mistakes in writing. Not only will it help you cope with "that-which" decisions, the book also encourages you to write clearly and simply.

Some organizations are fortunate enough to have a capable editor lurking among their staff members or volunteers. Others have a local editor or English teacher under contract to look at draft copy before it goes out. The result? Solid, readable releases that look like they're coming from a first-class organization.

Send out a hastily written release and you run the possibility of becoming the butt of newsroom banter. "Hey, Fred," your recipient calls out to a colleague. "Listen to this one from the art museum. It's a beaut!" Needless to say, you want to avoid that kind of media attention.

7

Keep Your Elevator Working

When I first heard the phrase "elevator message," I wondered what was so important about delivering a message while rising to the 15th floor. Then someone explained the idea was to be able to describe an organization's work to an outsider in the short space of an elevator ride. I've been a confirmed elevator man ever since.

I've known several masters of the elevator message. Each knew how to sound a few simple and powerful notes about his organization in such a way that every visitor left with an understanding of why the group mattered.

There is a knack to honing a simple message. The more tightly focused your niche, the easier it is to express who you are – witness groups from a local hospice to Habitat for Humanity. But even the sharpest niche can be subverted if you insist on saying too much in your message.

Given about 90 seconds, what would you say if asked, "What does Save Our Families do?"

You'll need to be direct and focused, answering just the basic questions:

- What does our organization do?

- Where is it heading?

- Why should anyone care?

The fact is, your time with reporters and visitors is fleeting. You want to impart key bits of memorable information that characterize your work.

Maybe you're a "camp for sick kids" that "transforms lives" by allowing youngsters to "play and be themselves for the first time." There is much more that leaders of the Hole in the Wall Gang Camps would want you to know. But, as I learned in working with the group, it is the beauty of allowing kids to be just kids that lies at the heart of the program.

Rest assured that Paul Newman, who founded the camps, could speak at length about the numbers of campers served, the careful medical management of the camps, the wonderful facilities that have been created for the kids, and the important respite that the kids' going away to camp offers stressed-out parents.

But you have to restrain yourself in the elevator – offering just enough to convey who you are and what's special about what you do, and no more.

Another way to think about an elevator message is to imagine a friend standing a hundred yards away on the other side of a river, and you have to shout for her to hear. What are the few declarative sentences you would be sure to get out if you were describing your organization? In the case of the Hole in the Wall Gang Camps, it would be:

We have camps for sick kids!

The experience transforms their lives!

The kids can play and be themselves – for the first time!

What do you want to shout for the world to hear? Figure that out, and you have the tight, focused message that will inform all of your publicity efforts.

8

Telling Your Story

We all love and need stories. Amid the chaos of life, nothing gives order and meaning as much as a well-told story. More to the point, stories grab people. Give a reporter a tale about a 75-year-old grandmother graduating from your business college, and he'll go for it every time.

You don't have to be a great storyteller to pitch a story to reporters. Just be sure you know all the facts – no surprises, please – and can provide the outline of why the story will make a great feature or broadcast segment.

Let's say yours is a community hospital with new outreach programs for inner-city families. Greater visibility will help boost patient numbers and perhaps scare up some new donors to meet the high costs of additional staff and facilities.

What is going on in your organization that is newsworthy? Sure, outstanding doctors and nurses are counseling families on drug abuse,

HIV/AIDS, and other issues. But they just sit still in rented office space talking across tables.

That is the lackluster setting. But what is the story dying to be told? You won't know until you contact the outreach staff and learn how the program is making a difference.

When you hear that 11-year-old Johnny's life was saved through counseling and rehab treatment that helped him break a cocaine habit, you're onto something. In fact, Johnny is bright and charming. He and the staff got along so well that Johnny and his family have invited doctors to their home to celebrate the boy's twelfth birthday.

I suspect you've already whipped out your cell phone to invite Channel 4 news to cover the party, which will be held in a neighborhood project right smack in the middle of an area served by the outreach program.

Amid the birthday cake, the smiling faces, and the banter between Johnny and a nurse, it becomes clear how important your outreach program is in helping families come back from the nightmare of addiction.

Your organization is filled with stories, no matter what your field. The challenge is to find them. And that's not as hard as you may think. Your program directors and specialists are on the front lines every day. They see remarkable things they probably take for granted.

9

The Cogent Example

When you're announcing a complex new program to the world, nothing brings it to life better than a vivid example. When we rolled out a new conservation effort called "Last Great Places" at The Nature Conservancy, we realized we'd have to explain our innovative "bioreserve approach."

If we didn't, that cockamamie term would simply get in the way of telling people about a promising new effort to conserve some of the country's most splendid natural areas.

What we needed were examples of how the Conservancy's work was changing. No longer would we buy small parcels of biologically rich land and fence them in. Now, we would design large preserves ("bioreserves") that protected land in places where human activities (from residential development to industry) were ongoing. Thus, both human activity *and* conservation would be compatible.

The approach involved working closely with business, government, and property owners in various locales to find ways to pursue conservation and still meet local economic needs. The only way to bring it home was to find a couple of stories. And so we did.

A staff writer was dispatched to the Texas Hill Country, one of the vast areas where we would be working, and interviewed individuals engaged in conservation there.

He produced an article about a handful of remarkable individuals, businesspeople and government leaders, who were already protecting wonderful natural resources from bat caves to the huge underground aquifer that supplies drinking water to San Antonio. The Conservancy would now bolster their efforts.

His story brought our program to life. You must strive to do the same with your own cogent examples that are specific, concrete, and make the abstract real.

If you serve disabled veterans, describe how your organization has helped transform the lives of two former soldiers. Now, you're not helping "disabled veterans," you're making a difference in the futures of Jimmy Rossman, 18, a private who lost a limb in the war in Iraq, and Linda Hill, 22, an officer and mother of two, who was partially paralyzed and must learn new ways to parent and earn a living.

Intriguing examples help sell a story. They allow a reporter to imagine what the story will look and feel like in a way that your formal announcement typically fails to do. The fact that you'll affect the lives of large numbers of people makes it all the more urgent that you tell him about one or two of them. Then, the journalist can visualize the story and convince his editor he should spend time on it.

10

Think Visually

Photographs make news. Sometimes, we wish they wouldn't. A finger in a bowl of chili at a fast food restaurant grabs national attention and scares away customers. Publicists at the same franchise would be delighted if a Presidential candidate dropped in for a burger and the photo appeared in news media across the country.

Your organization may not be a campaign stop any time soon. But keep an eye out. Photo possibilities unfold throughout the year. By keeping a digital camera handy, you can capture moments – either unexpected or choreographed – that win exposure in key media.

Which photos you take and how you use them will depend on which media are important to you. If you're trying to enhance ties to others in your field, a photo of leading experts visiting your program might interest a key professional journal.

The same picture will probably be of little interest to a large daily newspaper or general interest magazine. Of course if the visitors are from

North Korea – at a time when U.S. relations with that nation are strained – you may have media clamoring for that photo and much more.

As a student intern, I spent months working at the photo desk of the long-defunct *New York World Telegram*, a daily newspaper. I had little interest in photography. But I came to know the kinds of pictures the paper's editors favored. They showed action, depicted news events, and featured well-known, often pleasing-looking faces.

Increasingly, people rely strongly on images to absorb information. This is true for all of us, especially younger men and women, and it applies to print and broadcast media as well as the Internet.

Technology, fast-paced lives, and minimal attention spans all encourage this need for the visual. So act accordingly. With few exceptions, today's media are strong on graphics and light on text. Even *The New York Times* has been using color photos for years now.

Be mindful of opportunities to take unusual photographs. When the corporate executive who chairs your board visits one of your group's nature reserves, can he stand in a sweater and jeans on the back of a pickup truck? That's much more interesting than a studio picture of him in Brooks Brothers attire.

11

The People Factor

We all enjoy reading about other people. We like to listen to them, too, when they talk in interesting ways.

Your organization's program specialists may be greatly enamored of their work in arcane areas of economics or medicine that would stultify most of us. They aren't likely to make wonderful guests on TV talk shows.

But imagine for a moment how complex subjects often intrigue us when presented by someone who is articulate, lucid, and passionate about them.

The classic instance is Carl Sagan, the Cornell University astronomer, who enthralled millions of viewers in his popular PBS series, "Cosmos," and his bestselling books about the origins of the solar system.

Okay, there isn't a charismatic nerd on your staff. But look around. Quite often you'll find you have an individual at your organization who has a real knack for bringing his field to life, for making it clear and understandable, even exciting, to people who might otherwise find his work somewhat boring.

I recall one staff member at the Alcoholism Council of Greater New York. He could convey the drama and significance of family interventions in a way that made clear to listeners how vital it is to confront alcoholics and get them into rehab. A recovered alcoholic, he had been there himself. He could tell wrenching stories. And he was a great person to turn loose on reporters.

The medical director of a hospital where I consulted could recount heartwarming stories about dedicated doctors who had gone to great lengths to help their patients. In truth, he was a natural raconteur. We considered him a valuable resource for conveying the medical facility's tradition of caring to the media.

Unfortunately, many program gurus at nonprofits sit on high horses and refuse to explain their work. In my experience, this is especially true of scientists and other specialists who are privy to vast bodies of technical knowledge. They're fearful that if they "dumb down" information for the public, they'll sound like circus barkers.

In fact, you want such experts to discuss their work in plain English the way they would to intelligent friends outside their field. How would an oncologist explain his major findings to an accountant friend? What would a psychiatrist have to say to make the effects of a new drug understandable to a neighbor who manufactures carpets?

Like Carl Sagan, they'd have to talk in clear, simple language. They would have to talk *to* us, not down to us. They might even share their personal sense of wonder about the news-making development.

12

Make It Credible

In the 1980s, a member of philanthropist David Rockefeller's family created a nonprofit health agency to disseminate knowledge about mind-body health, i.e., how interactions between emotions and the body affect our health.

With an advisory board made up of prominent physicians, psychologists, and researchers from Harvard, Stanford, and other top universities, the Institute for the Advancement of Health examined the extraordinary claims made for the health-enhancing effects of diverse objects and techniques from crystal pendants to meditation and shared their findings.

The Institute faced quite a challenge. New Age remedies and approaches were growing enormously in popularity. At the same time, more than a few scientists scoffed at alternative medicine. Nevertheless, the Institute experts persisted in their work because they knew some mind-body interventions were beneficial.

To bolster its position, the Institute emphasized from the outset that it existed to provide information on *credible* approaches to improving health through mind-body techniques.

As a consultant, I worked with the group's clinicians and researchers, including Dean Ornish, M.D., who is now well known, but whose unusual program of lifestyle changes to reverse the effects of heart disease was then dismissed by most cardiologists. He has since demonstrated the efficacy of his approach through research published in leading medical journals.

Like the Institute, many nonprofits deal in areas that are controversial or off the beaten path. The more this is true of your group, the more you'll want to ensure the credibility of all the information you provide to the media. Be sure to separate out the hard facts and the speculation.

Let others send out the *in*credible stories. If the press falls for them (as it did, alas, when a group of UFO enthusiasts claimed to be cloning human beings some years ago), so be it. At least your organization isn't the one totally discredited.

When your staff takes positions or releases research that's contrary to received opinion, be certain of the accuracy of the information you're giving out. Check and double check. Cite recognized journals and experts. Make relevant data available to reporters who want it.

Be an utterly credible nonprofit and reporters will turn to you again and again, confident that yours is an organization they can trust.

13

Target Your Audience

You don't want to communicate with everybody, just the *right* people. Unfortunately, too many organizations keep churning out publicity material helter-skelter in the hope that exposure somewhere will count where it matters.

You may want to target a number of audiences. That's fine. But never think that communicating with the "general public" is going to hugely benefit your organization. You must determine the *specific* audiences that matter to you and devise a plan for reaching them.

Are you in the midst of a major fundraising campaign? From whom are you trying to raise money? Corporate executives, foundation leaders, and wealthy individuals tend to get their information from the elite media.

Is enrollment the key issue? If you want to attract students to your school, you'll want to get the word out in the media that prospective students turn to. Maybe it's some combination of websites, alternative newspapers, and television. Or maybe your students come from the Latino community exclusively, and you'll want to target Spanish-language media.

Are you trying to address the attacks of critics? In that case, getting your side of the story into the hands of journalists who have written about the critics would seem to be in order. Not to mention writers sympathetic to your cause.

Are you targeting older people? The poor? Yuppies? The wealthy? Young mothers? Whatever the group, some media will be far more effective in reaching them than others. A splash on CNN may be just what you need, or maybe not. A well-placed feature in *The Wall Street Journal* or *Business Week* may speak to your audience much more directly.

A placement on a daytime TV talk show won't help much if you're trying to reach business leaders. But it might be great for telling homemakers about your new water aerobics classes for moms and babies.

If you're uncertain about your audiences and can't afford a major marketing research effort, consider what some of my clients have done. They survey 100 donors or other supporters by mail and ask what these people think about the organization and aspects of its work. By doing some of the survey by phone, they're able to hear the tone and level of enthusiasm of the respondents.

Other organizations, trying to identify their key audiences, have been successful in enlisting the assistance of an M.B.A. marketing class at a local business school.

14

Where The Elite Meet

The wheelers and dealers in your community are critical to your publicity efforts. They are the people whose financial support and good graces sustain the work of your organization.

Where do they get their information? Are newspapers, radio or television their main source? Okay, you have those covered.

But maybe the powerful people you want to reach favor specialized media, including little-known newsletters or websites. For example, non-profit publishers are finding it just as important to gain attention at www.publisherslunch.com and www.thebookstandard.com as in *Publishers Weekly*.

These outlets may have limited audiences – but they reach precisely those that should know about your latest successes.

Your board members and other friends in leadership circles can help you determine in which media the elite meet. Ask them what sources they and their colleagues pay attention to. Don't waste time trying to break into a local business publication that no one takes seriously.

On the other hand, don't dismiss media outlets out of hand. I never thought *The Villager*, a free weekly in New York City, was very important. Then I learned that two aging and wealthy women on the board of one of my New York clients got all their news there. Suddenly, I had new respect for the paper. Most others on the board thought nothing was news until it appeared in *The New York Times*.

You can probably reach many leaders in the business, government, and donor communities through just a handful of media. Once you've identified those places, make every effort to cultivate relationships with key individuals.

15

Getting to Know You

There's a thin line between being polite and being aggressive in trying to win time with a reporter. Most often, it pays to be politely aggressive.

Some reporters and columnists are aloof. Others are far more approachable. They're the ones who will stay around to chat after a hearing, or who give talks at local press clubs and remain afterwards to talk with attendees. When such opportunities to cross paths with media people arise, try to have a few solid story ideas in hand.

The more familiar you are with a journalist's interests, the better your chance of getting to know him. While publicizing the work of the Alcoholism Council of Greater New York, I knew I could count on getting a meeting with reporters who were recovered alcoholics.

Similarly, over time you can learn which journalists have a deep and sometimes personal interest in your field, whether it's social work or the performing arts. If a leading health editor writes about her mother's ordeal with heart disease, you've found a new place to pitch a heart-related story in the future.

Others in your field may be willing to share information about the special penchants of journalists. And "Googling" the names of media people can prove useful. Online biographies often reveal personal angles that can relate directly to your cause. For example, if an editor has published a book about battered women, there's reason to think he might be interested in your shelter.

Some nonprofit publicists will simply pick up the phone and invite a reporter or editor to meet for coffee or lunch. Of course it helps to tie in the proposed get-together with a specific event (a new art exhibit, a sports event benefit, or some other fun and interesting occasion).

Whether that works will depend on the reporter. If he or she has some down time, and if you suggest you have a strong story idea, you may very well get your meeting.

A well-planned seminar for the press at your offices can also create a nice opportunity to cultivate reporters. For example, when employee drug testing was first introduced by corporations some years ago, I arranged a press seminar offering thoughtful legal and medical views on all aspects of the controversy.

Such seminars can be enormously useful to reporters, especially when they provide solid information on emerging issues.

The seminar should feature speakers who are noted authorities with information of strong interest to reporters covering your field. It's generally possible during breaks and other moments to chat informally with reporters and plant the seeds for future stories.

Something very nice happens when you do get to know a reporter and come through time and again with good story ideas for him. You begin to emerge from the pack in his mind. You're no longer just another nonprofit, but a valuable news source. You're a place where he can expect to get the quote or expert opinion he needs whenever he calls.

I can assure you that you'll be repaid for your effort.

16

Winning National Attention

Which public do you want to reach? Is your work of interest to the nationwide audience that watches network television, or only to the several thousand people who read your local daily?

Without a doubt, you want your messages to reach those who depend on local newspapers and radio and TV stations. These are the folks who participate in or support your programs. They are your students, clients, patients, or whatever. They also include voters whose opinions can affect your public funding.

As for the broad national public, what do you have to offer? If you're a nationally recognized organization with a major new study to announce, you'll do well to hold a press conference and invite all the big boys, from CNN and Fox News to *The Wall Street Journal.*

Otherwise, as a regional or local group, you'll want to be selective in approaching national media. You don't want to win a reputation as the small nonprofit that thinks its work in some town upstate will captivate top-flight journalists.

Be mindful, too, that national media reach highly segmented mass audiences. *Good Morning America*, *Oprah* and *The O'Reilly Factor* all appeal to distinctly different viewers. Do your homework and pitch to the right program.

Fortunately, many human interest stories have universal appeal. On several occasions, I placed stories with the *Associated Press* about students improving their lives through unusual programs at LaGuardia Community College. The features were picked up by dozens of the wire service's 1,500 newspaper subscribers.

One such story was about a special Saturday typing class for handicapped children. The sessions were taught by a likeable middle-aged businessman. It was obvious that he cared deeply about empowering kids with skills to do their homework or to enter the job market. His enthusiastic manner and patient interactions with the children created a moving AP story for the family pages of many newspapers.

When it comes to pitching ideas, I'm reminded of *The New York Times* reporter who was writing an article about the Gulf War when a public relations woman called and said she had a story right up his alley. The reporter said he was crazy busy and didn't have time to talk. She kept calling and pleading to make her pitch.

"Okay, go ahead," the reporter finally said.

"Thanks, I'll be brief," the woman said. "We're holding a contest, sponsored by an insecticide company, to find the world's biggest cockroach."

The reporter replied, "Here's my response, and *I'll* be brief," and hung up the phone.

To interest a top reporter at a national publication, you'll need a national story. Let's say that archeologists from your institution have discovered the earliest known remains of a Native American. That's something everyone will want to know about, no matter how tiny the source from which the news emerges. *Time* and *Slate* will do stories;

network TV crews will clamor to visit.

On the other hand, the appointment of a new program director at your nonprofit is of no interest to *The Los Angeles Times* – unless your group is located in that city, or the new director is a native, or he is a wanted fugitive from California. Even then they may not care.

This isn't to say an unusually appealing human interest story from your nonprofit might not be picked up nationally. (With articles widely available on the Internet, this happens more and more often when national reporters surf the Web in search of local examples for their stories.)

Nor does it mean you should ignore national columnists or beat reporters who have an interest in your field. But for the most part, unless something of great import has occurred in your small corner, you won't be working too often with national media.

The saving grace is that when national news breaks, whether in your local paper or on a website, it is picked up immediately around the country. So focus on the general media with an immediate interest in your work. Your successes there will garner the audience that matters the most.

17

Be Helpful Online

The first place a reporter is likely to look when writing a story about your organization is your website. What will she find there? If you must, lay on the hype and visual extravaganzas elsewhere on the website. In the press section, post only useful information.

Here's what a reporter will expect to find in the "For the Press" section of your website:

- Complete up-to-date contact information: name, title, phone number, cell number, and e-mail address. Give it prominent display.

- A good research tool that allows reporters to search the entire contents of the pressroom.

- Basic background on your organization: facts and figures on who you are, what you do, and where you're headed. Include relevant articles about your organization and links to other sources.

- Program areas: a summary of current work in each major division.

- History and profiles: this includes fact sheets, biographical sketches, and photographs.

- Annual reports: recent reports with financial figures.

- Press releases: an archive of recent releases.

- Other materials: speeches, newsletters, brochures, and other information as appropriate.

Most reporters appreciate a pressroom that's clean, up to date, easy to use, and quick to download. And on all your press releases and other media materials, remember to reference your online pressroom address.

18

Build Good Relations with the Media

While you don't need extensive media contacts to place a story, maintaining close and mutually respectful relationships with important reporters, editors, and producers is critical to a successful publicity program. Here are some behaviors that will foster good outcomes:

❏ Think like a reporter.

Journalists want a good *story*. That's all they want. They don't want to be your friend. They're not interested in writing promotional copy for you. They won't cover your organization just because you do good work. They want news and feature *stories*.

❏ Be prepared.

Reporters are generally bright, skeptical, and aggressive. Be prepared to answer questions. When pitching a story, have your facts straight and always have in mind several angles on the story. Say nothing to a reporter that you're not prepared to see on CNN (or whatever media outlet she represents) in the morning.

❐ Be direct.

Always make clear what you want from a reporter and why. Do you want him to cover an event, interview someone, attend a press seminar? Why should he bother, because you want him to? What's in it for *him* and his media outlet? Be able to say it all in a half minute or less.

❐ Be a valued source.

Build a reputation as someone who's helpful to journalists. If you know of a story that would probably interest an editor – or can offer valuable background on a topic in the news – call the editor and tell him. Do it even if your organization won't be mentioned. Your favor may be repaid later. For the same reason, don't hesitate to refer a reporter to experts at other organizations.

❐ Be professional.

Always act like a thorough-going professional. Return phone calls, get journalists the quotes they need, and respect their deadlines. Be courteous and remember that reporters must go away with a story.

When reporters start calling *you* for assistance on their stories, you will know that you've built good relations.

19

And Now The News

News has a life of its own. You come to the office one morning and find your prep school, which is about to launch a capital campaign, splashed across Page One of the local daily newspaper:

"Music Teacher Accused of Fondling Student."

News rears its ugly or handsome head every day – whether you like it or not. The roof of your facility collapses under the weight of drifting snow. A clerk embezzles money in your business office. Your board chair behaves scandalously in a nightclub. A student commits suicide. Your new president falsified his credentials.

Crises are rare. But they make great stories, especially when they offer the tabloid staples of sex, blood, or money. If that kind of news breaks at your organization, seek immediate assistance from an experienced public relations advisor.

Our focus in these pages is newsworthy stories of a gentler kind. They're not brimming with drama and conflict; but they do meet the old definition of news as something new, unusual, odd, or otherwise interesting.

As you think about the program areas for which you want more exposure, determine whether you have a story that fits into the following categories, which are generally of media interest.

❏ *Trends*

Interesting patterns among students, clients, patients, or others you serve may make an intriguing trend. The story might focus on the trend at your organization, or on your group as an example of a national trend. One recent story in many media focused on the spurt in enrollments in college forensics programs as a result of the popularity of "C.S.I." crime dramas on network television.

❏ *Seasons*

From the first day of spring to the winter holidays, seasons occasion a perennial need for feature copy. Are students building a giant snowman in front of the new student center?

❏ *Famous visitors*

Names will always make news. The right visitor to the right program at your organization can win extensive coverage. If a speaker addresses a hot topic in a new endowed lecture series, so much the better.

❏ *The first or last, the biggest or smallest*

There's always more human interest in the first woman president or the last chance ever to see a rare painting.

❏ *Research findings*

Studies that shed new light on health, politics, fashion, or other topics of wide public interest are newsmakers. The more provocative the findings, the better your chance of coverage.

❐ *Surveys*

Even informal surveys can produce fascinating stories. Has your heart group found that half of the adults surveyed in a downtown food court think high-cholesterol foods are good for you? That can be a TV news segment to kick off a health awareness campaign.

❐ *Advice*

Many nonprofits package the advice of staff experts on topics from family living to emerging cancer therapies. No matter what your field, you probably have staff experts who can offer helpful insights or tips on issues of the day.

❐ *New programs or people*

Is the English department offering a new class on novels about terrorism? Did your new security director live for 10 years as a Zen Buddhist monk in India? There may be media interest.

Without doubt, most organizations spend considerable time responding to the routine needs of reporters: a local radio station needs a quick quote; the town newspaper is doing a survey; a city magazine is highlighting adult classes for the fall.

That's all to the good. But organizations that tell their stories effectively take charge of their relationship with the news media. They regularly pitch news and feature possibilities. That way, they create news of the kind they want – and advance their specific publicity goals.

20

Make Your Pitch

The best way to place a story is to write a pitch letter. It must be brief – never longer than one page – and addressed to a specific reporter, editor, or news director. You don't have to tell the whole story, just enough to grab interest. The letter can accompany a press release or stand alone.

Your goal is simple: Convince the reporter that your story is interesting and will work well for her because it's tailored to the interests of her audience.

One of my early assignments in NYU's news bureau was to publicize the university libraries, a vast system that was always acquiring unusual and rare materials for its special collections. Research librarians thought every addition had the makings of a fascinating story. But I knew that talking to New York reporters about the incunabula of centuries ago would be a dead end.

Then one day Manhattan bookseller Francis Steloff donated her papers to the university.

Steloff was the charming owner of the Gotham Book Mart – a New York City literary institution she founded in 1920. There wasn't a reporter in town who didn't want to visit Steloff's landmark shop and interview her about James Joyce and the other experimental writers she had championed over the years. I played up that angle and wonderful feature stories ran in many major New York and national publications.

When making a pitch, a simple letter (*see Appendix A*) or e-mail is your best bet. If you must pitch by phone (the urgency of a story will sometimes require this), do so with care. Many reporters are understandably leery when someone calls to make a pitch. They've spent too much time listening to poorly conceived ideas.

Some tips for successful pitching:

- Keep your pitch tight, bright, and to the point.

- Make your first sentence count. The reporter may not read the second.

- Have your facts straight.

- Don't call several reporters at one media outlet to pitch the same story. If your key contact isn't interested, ask who else you might call. If you do pitch another reporter at the same place, let each know you have pitched the other.

- Be confident. You're doing a newsperson a favor by offering a story that readers or viewers will want.

You don't need press contacts to place stories. You only need a solid story and the right media outlet.

Go with your hunches. I once pitched a story about psychologist and publisher Glenn Ellenbogen and his humor magazine *The Jour-*

nal of Polymorphous Perversity. The journal spoofed traditional psychology journals with authentic-looking research studies on topics like "Psychotherapy of the Dead" and "Oral Sadism and the Vegetarian Personality." You get the idea. It was hilarious stuff, and my client was enlisting real-life psychologists, many of them well known, to write the satiric pieces.

Where to make my pitch?

At the time, *The Wall Street Journal* ran short offbeat features each day in a lower corner of the second front page. I had no contacts there, but I thought the story was a fit. So I called the paper, found out the name of the right editor, and mailed him a brief pitch letter with a copy of the magazine.

The result was a delightful feature that called the journal "a psychologist's answer to Mad Magazine." The psychologist has used *The Wall Street Journal* blurb in his advertising ever since.

21

Become a Go-to Person

Reporters aren't on the job long when they learn who they can rely on as news sources. Publicists who engage in drive-by pitches with little concern for the story needs of reporters go right to the bottom of the list. The professionals who are consistently responsive and helpful become the reliable sources.

My first boss at NYU's news bureau seemed to be on the phone with editors and reporters all the time. Granted, the university is a major New York institution. But those editors could just as easily have called other area colleges when working on stories. They called Bill Spencer at NYU. He understood their needs. He also understood the university. He could point a reporter to faculty members who made great copy, researchers with provocative new ideas, and bright students who were part of the latest trends.

Need a comment on the election? Writing a piece on dorm life? Want a local example for a campus activism story? Bill was the go-to guy. Moreover, if he didn't have what a reporter needed he would refer him to his counterpart uptown at Columbia. That way, Bill always delivered, as reporters knew he would.

Consider your own town. Which nonprofit leaders are usually quoted in stories involving health, education, nature, or the arts? Journalists often turn to the same places for a reason: some organizations know how to work smartly with the press. They make it their business to be useful in all ways.

Like Bill Spencer, you can become a go-to person in your field. It means learning as much as possible about your people and programs so you know where the expertise lies. It also requires your reading the latest books and articles so you understand exactly where your organization fits in to current trends.

Quicker than you think, reporters will soon realize you know what you're talking about. They'll begin to rely on your advice. Helping them won't always lead to stories about your group. But it'll certainly win you attentive media ears when the big must-place story comes along.

22

Be Consistent and Persistent

Woody Allen famously remarked that 90 percent of life is just showing up. The same is true of winning exposure in the news media – with the single caveat that you must keep showing up "as your usual self."

For many years I kept in touch with book and arts editors at media outlets in New York and elsewhere on behalf of several hundred independent book publishers who came together in Manhattan each year to exhibit and sell their books.

Most of the publishers were little known and oddly named – Painted Bride Quarterly, Rubber Stamp Press, and Fag Rag, for instance. Few could get their books on literary, political, feminist, gay, and other alternative topics into bookstores. That made our New York Book Fair an important way (in the pre-Internet 1970s) for the publishers to find readers and win media attention.

A gala, offbeat and slightly edgy event, the fair became a favorite of many reporters because it offered quirky human interest stories. And so editors were pleased when I called. They also knew I could provide background on small press publishing generally – a field on which few people keep tabs, since many such publishers are kitchen-table operations that come and go.

If all of a sudden I started pitching stories about mainstream publishers of romance or men's adventure titles, I would have surprised the same media contacts greatly. After all, they knew me as "the alternative books guy from the Book Fair" and here I was yakking about stuff sold on racks in drugstores.

Maybe your press contacts think of you as the "heart guy" or the "modern art guy." They've come to expect that you'll be bringing them stories from your area of expertise. This is your great advantage over the men and women pitching stories for multiple clients out of public relations agencies. You work a single strong patch of ground and, if you're any good, reporters will feel they can depend on you when it comes to that area.

As branders remind us, consistency helps make an organization memorable in the marketplace. That is most certainly true of the newsrooms at your target media outlets. Their floors are littered with ill-advised pitches from every oddball in town. They want to hear from reliable sources with real stories to tell.

Everything from your manner to your logo to your main messages should remain the same each time you come calling with a story idea. Much is unpredictable in the life of a reporter – but not you. You're rock solid. You're always there. You deliver. That earns you a prominent place in anyone's e-mail address book.

Be persistent in your pitching. Keep coming back with fresh ideas and don't give up. The last two pitches might not have worked at the local city magazine – in one case the editors felt your string quartet was "overexposed," and in the other they wanted to combine your organization with other performance groups in a larger feature on the new musical season – but that doesn't stop you.

Sometimes your ideas will be rejected. You may never know the reason why. Maybe the reporter's breakfast disagreed with him that day. Maybe his boss is tired of certain kinds of stories. Maybe your idea *is* lame. You're permitted a bomb now and then. Just don't make a habit of it.

23

Shooting Yourself in the Foot

When trying to place a story about your organization, there are some things you should never do ... even though sometimes you'll be mighty tempted:

• Don't call a reporter when you know he's on deadline. It will annoy him.

• Don't call to ask whether a reporter received your press release. (Better to simply pitch your story and while doing so remind him of the release.)

• Don't tell a reporter he's making a big mistake by not covering your event.

• Don't fail to answer questions. If *you* cannot provide answers, what is the reporter to think?

• Don't try to stop a reporter from using a good quote he obtained in an interview you arranged.

• Don't offer all-hype and no substance. You can't claim you've cloned the first human beings and then refuse to allow reporters to see the babies.

• Don't forget to have a Plan B. When you're away from the office, is there another spokesperson for your organization? If not, how will reporters get information?

• Don't treat a journalist like a good buddy. Never call him to say hi and chat.

• Don't send out news releases for the sake of getting a monthly quota of materials out.

• Don't make an unnewsworthy announcement because a board member has urged you to do so. Instead, use the occasion to educate your board member (ever so diplomatically) on the meaning of news and the importance of acting like a professional with the media.

24

Having Your Say

Many organizations find the op-ed, or opinion editorial, a highly effective way to express their views on an issue. Unlike a letter to the editor, the op-ed offers a chance for detailed discussion. Most often it provides a fresh perspective on the news.

Needless to say, the op-ed must work. It can't be self-serving puffery. Rather it must fill a gap in the public debate on an issue. So, for example, if a government official has made sweeping and wrongheaded statements about health care for the elderly, an organization with expertise in this area can provide an op-ed with solid numbers and thoughtful observations. This helps the paper offer balanced coverage and brings needed information to public attention.

Following the newspaper's style is important. Most op-eds run 500 to 800 words and offer a logical argument based on facts. If the information is fresh and unexpected - and submitted soon after the event or news story to which it responds - the article will stand an even greater chance of publication.

During the Reagan Administration's "Just Say No" campaign to encourage teenagers to avoid alcohol and drug abuse, I wrote and placed an op-ed in the *Chicago Sun-Times* about a new way to reach youths about their drinking. The article described the keen interest of a group of high school students in the relationship between alcohol use and their health and fitness.

When the telephone company in New York City decided to take the traditional "212" area code away from customers in several boroughs of the city, I wrote an op-ed for *The New York Times* about my experiences as a New York writer whose editors were confused about how to reach him – and whether he was in fact a New York writer – since he had a new area code of "718."

It was an unexpected and humorous take on matters in the news, and the *Times* editors had great fun with it: Under the headline "The Man from Area Code 718," they ran the article with an illustration of a man waiting for a phone call on the moon.

For an organization with something to say, the op-ed is a great vehicle with which to bring important messages to a broad audience. Once the article appears, it can be reprinted and mailed to supporters and others with a cover note.

25

Package Your Expertise

No matter how small, your organization has expertise people want and need. That's why your group is incorporated as a not-for-profit under section 501(c)3 of the Internal Revenue Code. You provide services that meet the public good.

If you're a small health agency, you have important advice to offer on heart disease or AIDS or the common cold. Organizations in the education field are fonts of wisdom on test-taking, doing homework, and on ways to prepare for careers.

Take advantage of your in-house expertise *in the areas that are a priority in your communications plan*. That may mean distributing a free booklet of advice on social drinking, as happened at the Alcoholism Council of Greater New York. Or it could mean creating a series of powerful public lectures on new developments in your field, then editing and collecting them for publication in a book underwritten by a foundation or corporate sponsor.

Every year, some organizations receive heightened media coverage when they release annual assessments of their fields. The American Lung Association makes a "State of the Air" report on the level of air pollution in each county and state. The National Trust for Historic Preservation announces America's "11 Most Endangered Historic Places." Consider issuing an annual "state of the field" report covering the field served by your organization.

The simplest gathering of information can win attention. Tip sheets on how to reduce urban sprawl, best ways to achieve financial success, how to avoid winter illnesses, or 10 ways to save your marriage, for instance, could come out of the mouths of experts at nonprofits large and small. The public craves useful information. Reporters like experts who have it to offer. Why not make your organization a source for that expertise?

Advice and information can become the basis for free booklets, op-ed pieces, TV and radio appearances, and more. Radio in particular is an excellent outlet when you have an expert with something to say. The venues range from National Public Radio to the scores of local and syndicated programs around the country that bring guests into conversations by telephone.

The work of some organizations lends itself to more ambitious packaging – in a book. Depending on your goals and the size of the potential audience, the book can be self-published or brought out by a regional or national book publisher.

The main question is: Do you have material for a compelling book? Can you transform your expertise and experiences into an outstanding regional guide to the outdoors, a children's book based on themes in your field, or an engrossing collection of interviews with people you have served?

I once developed a benefit anthology that consisted of original writing about landscapes where The Nature Conservancy works in the U.S., Latin America, and Asia. The contributors included Barbara

Kingsolver, Carl Hiaasen, Paul Theroux, Louise Erdrich, William Least Heat-Moon, and other nature and outdoor writers.

Each spent time at a favorite place (with travel paid for by the publisher's advance money) and provided a response in the form of a donated essay. The collection, *Heart of the Land: Essays on Last Great Places* (Pantheon), inspired a series of CBS Television reports and tied in nicely with an ongoing capital campaign.

Warning: Enthusiastic trustees or others may urge you to do a book. Such projects can be complex and time-consuming. Before you do anything, discuss the book idea with a bookseller or regional publisher. There may be no audience for what you want to do.

26

Waging Campaigns

I once worked with the executive director of an alcoholism prevention agency in New York City on a health awareness campaign. It was aimed at encouraging social drinkers to consider the possible health effects of their alcohol use.

The campaign wasn't opposed to drinking. Indeed, the executive director was a social drinker. Rather, the campaign argued that just as cholesterol, for example, can affect a person's health depending on personal health predispositions, so can use of beer, wine, or hard liquor.

The campaign tried to help health-conscious drinkers understand how alcohol use might affect an existing health problem – from bone disease to a heart condition – or relate to concerns over personal appearance or weight. At the same time it made clear that alcohol's possible effects ran a gamut – from broken veins or dehydration in some people to the terrible disease known as alcoholism in others.

That is fairly nuanced stuff. I was impressed by how much the executive director had accomplished – without any public relations staff – before I signed on to help.

The centerpiece of the initiative was a small, attractively designed booklet called "A Health and Fitness Guide to Alcohol." Bright, positive, and non-threatening on a sensitive subject, the guide was offered free of charge to anyone requesting a copy. Its production had been underwritten by a donor. Copy and design had been donated by a board member's firm. All the agency had to do was promote the availability of the free booklet.

The executive director sent a two-page press release and a copy of the booklet to major local and national media, with an emphasis on health editors and service magazines. The unusual new guide was covered in diverse media outlets, with the Associated Press moving a feature story, and – best of all – "Dear Abby" urging readers of her nationally syndicated column to obtain and read the booklet.

The response was phenomenal. Thousands of individuals and organizations requested the guide. The U.S. State Department and Fortune 500 corporations ran excerpts in internal publications and in some cases began using the booklet in employee health programs.

That was the beginning. The free guide opened the door for regular print and broadcast interviews with agency staff as well as a handsomely produced series of public service spots on a major New York TV station. The spots featured a health reporter asking true-or-false questions about alcohol use and personal health. Ultimately, the health awareness effort became the basis for the book *You Are What You Drink* (Villard, 1989), which I wrote with the executive director.

If your agency engages in an informational campaign, always look for a simple and fresh way to open the door to your audience. This is doubly important if your subject matter is complex or daunting. If you can link your campaign to some pressing current public concern, so much the better. The prevention agency's free guide appeared at the peak of a boom of interest in health and fitness.

In another instance where packaging information in a new and accessible way proved a powerful technique for sparking a campaign, the Union of Concerned Scientists (UCS) decided not long ago to educate people about what they could do to combat global warming.

Leaders of the Cambridge-based environmental group were concerned that many citizens felt overwhelmed and helpless in the face of warnings about the dire effects of greenhouse gases on the Earth. So they created an unusual 12-page booklet, *Common Sense on Climate Change: Practical Solutions to Global Warming.*

As a consultant to the project, I was taken by the group's positive, upbeat message that there are simple, practical solutions that can slow global warming. Too often, organizations emphasize the negative aspects of situations they're trying to remedy and fail to demonstrate how people can engage in positive action.

The UCS brochure outlined five "sensible steps" readers could take, ranging from smart auto purchases to efficient energy use at home and work. The information was specific, concrete and empowering. Readers even learned how many tons of heat-trapping gases would be kept out of the air each year as a result of each suggested action.

The program of story placements, press events, and TV appearances by UCS staff based on the booklet won widespread attention for the fresh and powerful message that each of us *can* do something about climate change.

As the foregoing examples show, tapping into the pressing concerns of target audiences can be the key to successful information campaigns. People will pay attention to even complex messages if you answer the question, *What's in it for me?*

27

Staying Fresh

Never lose passion for your good cause. Your enthusiasm is what drives you to keep alert for stories to share with reporters. It's easy to grow stale, especially after you've been through several years of the cycle of news-making events at your organization.

One way to stay interested is to get out the door regularly and visit the wards, classrooms, galleries, shelters, theaters, playgrounds, and other places where the wonder of your organization's work touches the lives of people. When you get there, watch and listen. It can be completely reinvigorating to be at the heart of things and see your mission in action.

For my part, tropical rainforests were just facts and figures until one day I traveled to Panama and climbed thousands of feet up into a dense jungle teeming with monkeys, birds and other wildlife. After seeing that astonishing place and meeting indigenous people determined to save it, I felt a heightened appreciation for the stories I was telling for a conservation client.

In the same way, recovery from drug and alcohol abuse remained an abstraction for me until the night I visited a counseling session for a large group of addicts who had recently come out of a detoxification unit. Their wrenching stories of their lives on drugs reminded me of the importance of a client's programs.

Staff members at many organizations manage to stay excited about their work in diverse ways.

Many get to know their interns and volunteers. These people toil at your organization for little or no compensation. Why? As students or retired people, they could find other things to do. Yet something excites them about the place.

Sometimes, at their own organizations, staff members put in extra time working as volunteers so that they can get a "hands on" feel for various programs.

Others spend time around articulate colleagues – the ones who breathe fire and have dedicated their lives to the field.

I've also noticed that those who retain a commitment to their cause – no matter how overworked their days may be – find ways to relax away from the job. They take their annual vacation. And while away, they listen when other vacationers tell them about the wretched things they do for a living. That reminds them why they care about their organization and publicizing its work.

Nonprofit publicists can't afford to have "just another day at the office." They must keep attuned to the magic of their agencies' work. From that powerful place, they can tell their group's story.

28

Publicity Checklist

Some basic systems and resources are essential to conducting an effective publicity effort. Some you will want to act on immediately. Others can be developed gradually, as time and budget allow.

❏ Have you created a publicity plan and key messages?

❏ Have you identified your target audiences?

❏ Do you have up-to-date mailing lists and contact information for key media outlets?

❏ Do you have the latest directories of local and national media outlets?

❏ Have you flagged dates on your calendar that are important to your media goals?

❑ Do you know the deadlines of key reporters, editors, and producers?

❑ Are you in regular touch with your press contacts?

❑ Are you keeping clips of your media placements and circulating them to selected board and staff members?

❑ Are you watching the stories covered by key media so you know their interests and needs?

❑ Do you keep in regular touch with program directors and people who use your organization's services to be sure you're aware of the latest developments?

❑ Are you networking with colleagues at other organizations in your area to share information on media outreach possibilities?

❑ Do you have a process for editing and obtaining in-house approvals for copy that will be sent to the media?

❑ Are the background sheets on your organization up to date?

❑ Have you developed and circulated an annotated list of experts who are willing to speak to the press?

❑ Do you have a press section on your website, is it easy to use, and does it offer current information useful to reporters?

29

The Secret

By now you know the secret: Anyone can do publicity work. You don't need extensive training or experience to be successful. But you do have to recognize a news or feature story when you see it, and be able to place it effectively with the news media.

It helps to be a former journalist or to have extensive knowledge of the field in which your organization has carved a niche, or both. But it's not required. If you're bright, creative, and a quick study, you can help achieve your group's marketing goals.

Let me assure you in closing that the rewards can be immensely gratifying – for both you and your organization

Significant media coverage can generate new opportunities, new funding, and new recognition for your organization. It can reach the population you serve. In a word, it can help you achieve mission success.

Your personal job satisfaction increases as more people realize the importance of your organization. Your successes can also benefit your career. But I suspect that like many of us you grew up wanting to save the world. In that case, your successes will produce a greater satisfaction. It is the quiet knowledge that you have given powerful voice to actions that educate, inspire, restore, nurture, heal, conserve, or otherwise improve the quality of all our lives.

Go ahead. Attract the attention your cause deserves.

APPENDIX

SAMPLE PITCH LETTER

Dear Mr./Ms. Producer:

The Surgeon General has declared obesity a national epidemic. But here at Drake University, we're showing that healthy new behaviors have a strong chance of reversing the trend.

<u>Twenty adults in our Diet and Fitness Center program have lost an average of 40 pounds and kept the weight off for more than two years. We think their stories will make a strong feature piece for the Argosy's health section.</u>

The patients — all from the tri-state area — come from diverse backgrounds. They include Sally Grimes, a 38-year-old homemaker, who lost all the weight she had gained in a recent pregnancy; Sal Orsini, a 61-year-old writer who dropped to 260 pounds from 285, lowering his blood pressure significantly; and Ron Dewey, a 30-year-old account executive whose 50-pound weight loss has brought his diabetes under control.

"I wouldn't have believed this was possible — and yet I have done it," says Orsini, who now engages in aerobic walking for an hour daily. "And I am still able to eat all my favorite foods."

If you are interested, I can arrange an interview with Dr. Claude Johnson, medical director of the Diet and Fitness Center and author of the widely hailed book, *Sensible Eating and Exercise for Sensible Living.* More than a half dozen of our 20 successful patients, including those mentioned above, have also agreed to be interviewed.

I believe a story with photos of these men and women as they exercise, eat, and go about their daily lives will be informative and appealing to your readers.

Thanks very much for your consideration. I will call you shortly.

Best wishes,

Name
Title

P.S. Enclosed is a brief fact sheet on the Diet and Fitness Center.

THE TOOLBOX

Here are tools you will use frequently or only occasionally, depending on the nature of your organization. You won't go wrong if you keep one question in mind: How can I be most useful to reporters?

• *The pitch letter*

You'll use this regularly. Always make it a one-page grabber. (No attachments, please, if you use e-mail; media outlets want to stay free of viruses.)

• *The press release*

Use it for more routine announcements. Keep releases as short as possible

• *The press kit*

A folder with basic background materials on your organization is always useful. Limit your use of special press kits to major occasions, such as graduations, campaign rollouts, and building dedications.

• *The op-ed piece*

The by-lined opinion piece is a natural for issue-oriented organizations. As appropriate, they can be placed in publications in different geographic areas that don't compete for readers.

• *The press conference*

Only *major news* warrants a formal press conference. Use them sparingly, and *never* hold one simply to please a board member or other significant insiders. You'll only wind up having to ask staff members to fill empty seats at the last minute.

• *The press seminar*

Discussions that bring together a few leading experts in your field – both staff and outsiders – can be useful for reporters. If the event generates good story ideas, so much the better. Make sure your seminar focuses on hot topics and includes top-notch speakers.

• *The celebrity spokesperson*

Attractive figures draw the press, to be sure. But be careful: I worked with a well-known actress at one organization whose manager was demanding, unpleasant, and dreaded by staff members. Always consider costs and benefits before involving Hollywood.

• *The letter to the editor*

Having placed my share, I implore you: keep letters on point and as short as possible. Offer a compelling view they *have* to publish.

IDENTITY CHECK

There's a simple way to inventory and identify your organization's strengths so that you can better target your publicity efforts. With the assistance of trusted board and staff members, take these three simple steps to discover the essence of your group's work.

READ

Find out what your group has been telling the world about itself by examining a stack of your printed materials of the past several years. These will usually consist of annual reports, newsletters, press releases, brochures, and other marketing pieces. As you scan the pages, ask yourself:

- What do the text and graphics say about the organization?
- Are we portrayed as young, old, diverse?
- Do we serve one central need?
- Is the need growing?
- Are we expanding?
- Are we cutting edge?
- Are we going off in many directions in our programming?

The answers to these questions will reveal the messages you have actually been conveying about your organization. The rest of your investigation will uncover what changes, if any, you must make to those messages.

OBSERVE

Spend time with your organization's clients – in the places where your programs are offered. Watch the situation and note what it tells you about your group.

- Are participants engaged and excited?
- Are program leaders outstanding or mediocre?
- What does the situation demonstrate about the importance of your services?

Ask a few participants about themselves and what brought them to the program. Start them talking informally. What do they like best about the program, and why? How does it matter to them?

LISTEN

Make a list of 10 people who know your organization well. They can include board and staff members as well as funders. Ideally you want to meet with each of them briefly and pose several questions:

- What are the three things that come to mind when you think about our organization?
- What's the one thing you wish people better understood about us?
- What is our greatest contribution to the field?
- What do you dislike about us?
- Has our role changed in recent years? How?
- Are we meeting new needs?

If your organization's strength and its identity have remained constant, you'll find the messages you've been using in your printed material still apply today. If not, use the insights gained in your visits to revise the way you talk about your group.

THE MARKET SURVEY

The market survey is an effective way to learn more about your target audiences. If you can't afford a marketing firm – which will offer the most scientifically valid results – consider conducting an informal mail or phone survey.

Here's what several of my clients have done:

1) Develop a survey questionnaire of about 10 questions (any more and people won't take the time to respond). Multiple choice questions work best.

For example, a community education program might ask:

Which kind of educational format do you prefer?
[ ] Seminar
[ ] Workshop
[ ] Lecture

In which area would you like to see expanded programming?
[ ] Arts and humanities
[ ] Career education
[ ] Health and wellness

Which best describes you?
[ ] Employed outside the house
[ ] Student
[ ] Homemaker
[ ] Other, please specify _____.

2) Generate a random sampling of addresses or phone numbers to use in the survey. These should be developed from lists of donors, members, prospective clients, or whatever audience you're surveying. The phone survey has the major advantage of allowing the interviewer

to hear and make note of the tone of the respondent's voice.

3) Conduct the survey. If doing so by mail, provide a stamped, reply envelope. If using the phone, read each question and take notes on the responses. Refrain from offering any comments that could affect the participant's opinion.

4) When conducting the survey by phone, be sure to speak with the specific person on your list. If mailed surveys are sent back under another name, discard.

5) Compile the results. Show the number of people responding to the choices for each question as well as a selection of the most useful comments.

Some organizations enlist the help of graduate marketing students when conducting a market survey. At no cost, these students help develop the questions and the random sampling.

Needless to say, the more time spent on planning the survey, the likelier you are to obtain meaningful information about your audience.

ACKNOWLEDGMENTS

In writing this book, I have drawn on several decades of experience as a writer and publicist for many good causes, both large and small. I want to thank all of my nonprofit clients for the privilege of working with them. They make this world a better place.

I received my initial grounding in communicating for nonprofits during my dozen years on the advancement staff of New York University, especially in Bill Spencer's news office. Bill ran a first-class shop. I am deeply indebted to him and to others from those wonderful days at Washington Square – Jack Wilson, Bob Terte, and Fritz Witti – who taught me how to tell the story of a nonprofit. Everyone should have such generous teachers.

As always, my wife, Dusty, has been a source of strength and encouragement.

Finally, a special thanks to Jerry Cianciolo at Emerson & Church, Publishers, for his advice and patience, and for the pleasure of working with him.

ABOUT THE AUTHOR

Joseph Barbato is president of Barbato Associates, a consulting firm whose clients include many of the nation's leading nonprofits. He has worked as a writer, editor and director in the public relations and development offices of several institutions, including New York University, The Nature Conservancy, and the City University of New York.

He is the author or coauthor of six earlier books, two of which were featured on "The Today Show." His most recent book, *How to Write Knockout Proposals* (Emerson & Church, Publishers), won a starred review from *Publishers Weekly*, which called it "sound, clear and to the point ... a lifeline for anyone who has ever struggled to write a grant proposal."

Barbato has worked on both sides of the media pitch. He has been a writer, columnist, and editor for many magazines, and a contributor to *The New York Times*, *USA Today*, *Smithsonian*, *The Washington Post*, and the *Chronicle of Higher Education*. His syndicated features appeared for many years in the *Los Angeles Times*, the *Chicago Sun-Times*, the *San Francisco Chronicle*, *Newsday*, and other newspapers.

As a publicist, he has won new recognition for the people and programs of many nonprofits in education, health care, and other fields. As publicity director for the New York Book Fair, an annual publishing event held in Madison Square Garden, Lincoln Center, and other Manhattan locations in the 1970s and 80s, he helped bring national attention to the work of hundreds of independent book publishers from throughout the country.

His consulting firm provides editorial services to the advancement programs of many nonprofit institutions. Clients have included M.I.T., the U.S. Fund for UNICEF, Environmental Defense, the Westport Playhouse, the University of Maryland Medical Center, and the Hole in the Wall Gang Camps.

Barbato has presented seminars on writing for many organizations, including Duke University, the Rainforest Alliance, the National Trust for Historic Preservation, the Kresge Foundation, and the Grant Center in Memphis.

He earned his B.A. in journalism and his M.A. in American studies at New York University, where he served in his senior year as campus correspondent for *The New York Times*.

Barbato is a member of the Association of Fundraising Professionals, the Authors Guild, and the National Book Critics Circle. He has served twice as president of Washington Independent Writers, an organization of 1,800 journalists, authors, and other writers in the nation's capital.

Barbato can be reached at www.barbatoassociates.com.

INDEX

Also by Emerson & Church, Publishers

The Ultimate Board Member's Book

A 1-Hour Guide to Understanding and Fulfilling
Your Role and Responsibilities • *Kay Sprinkel Grace*

Here is a book for *all* nonprofit boards.
• Those wanting to operate with maximum effectiveness
• Those needing to clarify exactly what their job is, and,
• Those wanting to ensure that all members – novice and veteran alike – are 'on the same page' with respect to roles and responsibilities.

It's all here in jargon-free language: how boards work, what the job entails, the time commitment, the role of staff, serving on committees and task forces, fundraising responsibilities, conflicts of interest, group decision-making, effective recruiting, board self-evaluation, and more.

Fund Raising Realities
Every Board Member Must Face

A 1-Hour Crash Course on Raising Major Gifts
for Nonprofit Organizations • *David Lansdowne*

More than 50,000 board members and development officers across America have used the book, *Fund Raising Realities*, to help them raise substantial money – in both good and bad economies.

In fact, David Lansdowne's classic has become *the* fastest selling fundraising book in America.

It's easy to see why. Have your board spend just one hour with this eyeopening gem and they'll come to understand virtually everything they need to know about raising big gifts. Nothing more, nothing less.

Asking

A 59-Minute Guide to Everything Board Members,
Volunteers, and Staff Must Know to Secure the Gift • *Jerold Panas*

It ranks right up there with public speaking. Nearly all of us fear it. And yet it's critical to our success as board members and staff. Asking for money. It makes even the stout-hearted quiver.

But now comes the book, *Asking*, and short of a medical elixir it's the next best thing for emboldening you, your board members, and your volunteers to ask with skill, finesse ... and powerful results.

Nearly everyone, regardless of their persuasive ability, can become an effective fundraiser by following Jerold Panas' step-by-step guidelines.

Also by Emerson & Church, Publishers

Big Gifts for Small Groups
A Board Member's 1-Hour Guide to Securing Gifts
of $500 to $5,000 • *Andy Robinson*

If yours is among the tens of thousands of organizations for whom six- and seven-figure gifts are unattainable, then *Big Gifts for Small Groups* is just the ticket for you and your board.

Robinson is the straightest of shooters. There literally isn't one piece of advice in this book that's glib or inauthentic. As a result, board members will instantly take to the book, confident the author isn't slinging easy bromides.

They'll learn everything they need to know from this one-hour read: how to get ready for the campaign, whom to approach, where to find them; where to conduct the meeting, what to bring with you, how to ask, how to make it easy for the donor to give, what to do once you have the commitment – even how to convey your thanks in a memorable way.

Fundraising Mistakes that Bedevil All Boards
A 1-Hour Guide to Identifying and Overcoming
Obstacles to Your Success • *Kay Sprinkel Grace*

Fundraising mistakes are a thing of the past. Or, rather, there's no excuse for making a mistake anymore. And that goes for board members, staff, novice, or veteran.

If you blunder from now on, it's simply evidence you haven't read Kay Sprinkel Grace's book, *Fundraising Mistakes that Bedevil All Boards (and Staff Too)*, in which she exposes *all* of the costly errors that thwart us time and again.

The appeal of this book is that in one place it gathers and discusses the "Top 40" miscues – some readily apparent, others more subtle.

Just as anyone involved in journalism should own a copy of Strunk and White's, *The Elements of Style*, anyone involved in fundraising should have *Fundraising Mistakes that Bedevil All Boards (and Staffs)* by their side.

How Are We Doing?
A 1-Hour Guide to Evaluating Your Performance
as a Nonprofit Board • *Gayle L. Gifford*

Until now, almost all books dealing with board evaluation have had an air of unreality about them. The perplexing graphs, the matrix boxes, the overlong questionnaires. It took only a thumbing through to render a judgment: "My board's going to use this? Get real!"

Enter Gayle Gifford. Inhale the fresh air. See the ground break. Watch the clutter clear. This nationally respected trainer has pioneered an elegantly simple and enjoyable way for your board to evaluate *and* improve its overall performance.

It all comes down to answering a host of straightforward questions – questions that as Graham Greene would say, get to "the heart of the matter."

Copies of this book, and others from the publisher,
are available at discount when purchased in quantity
for boards of directors, volunteers, or staff.

Emerson
& Church
PUBLISHERS

P.O. Box 338 • Medfield, MA 02052
Tel. 508-359-0019 • Fax 508-359-2703
www.emersonandchurch.com